DIVE INTO SEO

QNimate

© QNimate 2014, qnimate.com

All rights reserved. No part of this publication may be reproduced or redistributed in any form without the prior written permission of the publishers.

Table Of Contents

1. Introduction to SEO
    1.1 What is SEO?
    1.2 Benefits of SEO
    1.3 Types of SEO

2. HTML Tags
    2.1 Title Tag
    2.2 Meta Description Tag
    2.3 Heading Tags
    2.4 Bold and Italic Tags

3. Optimizing Images
    3.1 Alt Attribute
    3.2 File Size
    3.3 Image File Name

4. Indexing and Crawling
    4.1 Sitemaps
    4.2 Robot Exclusion Protocol

5. Page Speed
    5.1 Web Caching
    5.2 Code Minfication
    5.3 Compressing

6. Redirection and Duplicate Content
    6.1 URL Redirection
    6.2 Types of Redirection
    6.3 HTTP Redirection
    6.4 HTML Redirection
    6.5 301 Redirect
    6.6 302 Redirect
    6.7 303 Redirect
    6.8 308 Redirect
    6.9 HTTP Refresh Header
    6.10 Refresh Meta Tag
    6.11 Duplicate Content in Websites
    6.12 Duplicate Content Problems
    6.13 Solution to Duplicate Content
    6.14 Canonical Link as Solution
    6.15 HTTP Redirection as a Solution
    6.16 Robots as Solution

7. Web Caching
    7.1 What is Web Caching?
    7.2 Advantage of Web Caching
    7.3 Systems using Web Caching
    7.4 CDNs, Proxies and Browsers
    7.5 Calculation of Expiration Time
    7.6 Web Caching in Search Engines

8. Pagination
    8.1 What is Pagination?
    8.2 Solving Pagination Problems
    8.3 Leave it to Search Engines

      8.4 Canonical Link
      8.5 Next and Previous Link
      8.6 Canonical Link to First Page

9. Authorship
      9.1 What is Google Authorship?
      9.2 Google Authorship - Method One
      9.3 Google Authorship - Method Two
      9.4 SEO Impact of Authorship

10. Local and National SEO
      10.1 What is Local Search?
      10.2 On-Site Optimization
      10.3 National SEO
      10.4 Local SEO

11. Multi-Language and Multi-Currency SEO
      11.1 What is Multi-Language SEO?
      11.2 URL Structure
      11.3 Search Problems
      11.3 Alternate Link

12. Pagerank
      12.1 What is Pagerank
      12.2 Building Backlinks
      12.3 nofollow

13. Miscellaneous
      13.1 Using Deprecated Tags

13.2 Responsive Website
13.3 Use of Underscores
13.4 Flash Content
13.5 Social Sharing
13.6 Spelling and Grammer
13.7 Guest Posting
13.8 Use of Themes
13.9 Domain Age
13.10 Paid Backlinks

14. SEO Tools

Introduction To SEO

In this chapter we will look at what SEO is? And what are its benefits? And then we will jump into different types of SEO. By the end of this chapter you will have a basic idea about why you need SEO? and how is it going to help your website.

What is SEO?

SEO stands for Search Engine Optimization. SEO is a process of affecting the visibility of website or a webpage in organic search result. This is done to get a higher rank in organic search result.

SEO is not only limited to document search. Its also applied to image search, local search and all other kinds of searches.

Benefits of SEO

Some benefits of SEO are:

- SEO helps to get more organic traffic to website. You don't have to spend money on advertising to get traffic.

- SEO helps to build your brand. If you website is listed above other websites then you website brand is more valuable.
- If you website is dependent on advertising revenue then organic traffic is the best source to increase the revenue.
- If you advertising your website to get traffic then the traffic is not permanent. But organic traffic is permanent.

The above listed points are some benefits of SEO. Every website needs SEO.

Types of SEO?

SEO has traditionally divided into two main areas; on-page optimisation which covers what can be done on the pages of the website itself, and off-page optimisation which covers activity that takes place out side your website.

On-page and off-page SEO are equivalently important to get a better ranking in search result. On-page is mostly done during website creation. But off-page SEO is done continuously throughout the life time of website.

HTML Tags

There are certain HTML tags whose content are used by search engines to match the user queries and also to understand the content of the webpage. These basic tags can must be used whenever possible.

Title tag

Title tag defines the title of the web page. Title is visible to the user in browser window and also in search result. The length of title shouldn't exceed 70 characters.

Make sure that title contains words what users search for. You title should be attractive and contain all keywords. It should convey the real purpose of your document.

Markup for title looks like this:

```
<head>
    <title>QNimate</title>
</head>
```

Title tag should be placed inside the head tag.

Title tags is displayed in search result like this

QNimate
qnimate.com/ ▼
QNimate is a blog maintained by Narayan Prusty. Posts are mostly focused on programming.

The first line is the title displayed in Google search result.

Meta description tag

Meta description tag is used to provide a description of the document. The length of description shouldn't exceed 160 characters.

Description should be easy to read and should be clear about the motive of the document. Description should contain words that users search for.

Search engines display the description in search result.

Markup for meta description tag is:

```
<head>
    <meta name="description" content="QNimate is a blog maintained by Narayan Prusty. Posts are mostly focused on programming." />
</head>
```

The meta description tag should be placed inside head tag.

Search engines display meta description tag like this

QNimate
qnimate.com/ ▾
QNimate is a blog maintained by Narayan Prusty. Posts are mostly focused on programming.

Description starts in the third line.

Heading tags

Making use of heading tags in webpage is a good practice. Heading tags should be used to display headings and sub-headings inside a webpage. Search engines give a lot of importance to heading tags.

Heading tags should contain keywords. Its better to have only one h1 tag in webpage. We can have multiple number of h2, h3, h4, h5 and h6 tags. These tags should be used in order. Search engines match search queries with the heading tags to find matching documents.

Markup for heading tag is:

```
<body>
<h1>The main heading</h1>
<h2>Sub-heading of main heading</h2>
<h3>Sub-heading of h2</h3>
</body>
```

Heading tags can be placed anywhere inside body tag.

Bold and Italic tags

You should use bold and italic tags to highlight text in webpage. It helps users to read through important points in the document and also helps search engines to index important text of your webpage.

Bold and Italic tags have a very little SEO impact. There is no harm in using them therefore they should be used whenever possible.

Markup for bold and italic tag is:

```
<body>
<b>This is bold text</b>
<i>This is italic text</i>
</body>
```

Bold and italic tags can be placed anywhere inside body tag.

Optimizing Images

Optimizing images helps users to find images of your website in image search. Image search also drives traffic into your website. You need to explicitly provide information about your images to search engines.

Alt attribute

Humans can see and understand images but search engines cannot. Search engines use the alt attribute of img tag to understand the images. Search engines match the search queries with the text in alt attribute. Alt attribute value must contain keywords identifying the objects image.

Markup for alt attribute:

```
<img src="http://qnimate.com/qnimate-logo.png" alt="qnimate logo" />
```

File size

Images with large file size make the webpage load slower. Search engines don't like pages which load slow. Make sure that your images file sizes is as small as possible without sacrificing quality. There are many online tools available to compress the image file size.

Try to make sure that image dimension is same as image display area dimension. Having images large than the display area is unnecessary because it decreases the image display quality due to compression and also file size is more than needed.

Use .png format only when transparency in image is required. Otherwise its better to use .jpeg format.

Image file name

Make sure than image file name is descriptive. Its as important as alt attribute. Search engines match the search query with the name of the file. Don't make file name length to be too big.

Indexing and Crawling

You can control how search engines index and crawl your website. Ofcourse all factors cannot be controlled, you can only control those things which don't have a negative impact on search engines and are not spammy for search engines.

Sitemaps and Robots exclusion protocol are various ways to control how search engines crawl and index your website.

Sitemaps

A sitemap is a XML or HTML file which is provided by the website to search engines. Sitemap contains list of all webpages of the website. A sitemap helps search engines to plan a crawling strategy. There are a lot more information you can provide using sitemaps which will help search engines to crawl and index webpages of your website.

Sitemaps can be submitted to search engines manually. or you can place them in the root directory so that search engines will find it implicitly.

Its not compulsory to use a sitemap. Its better to use it if webpages in your website are not properly linked or has dynamic content.

An example of XML sitemap is:

```
<?xml version="1.0" encoding="UTF-8"?>
<urlset
    xmlns="http://www.sitemaps.org/schemas/sitemap/0.9"
    xmlns:xsi="http://www.w3.org/2001/XMLSchema-instance"
    xsi:schemaLocation="http://www.sitemaps.org/schemas/sitemap/0.9
        http://www.sitemaps.org/schemas/sitemap/0.9/sitemap.xsd">
<url>
 <loc>http://qnimate.com/</loc>
 <changefreq>weekly</changefreq>
 <priority>1.00</priority>
</url>
<url>
 <loc>http://qnimate.com/feed/</loc>
 <lastmod>2014-06-02T17:43:02+00:00</lastmod>
 <changefreq>weekly</changefreq>
 <priority>0.80</priority>
</url>
<url>
 <loc>http://qnimate.com/create-a-awesome-raining-effect/</loc>
 <changefreq>weekly</changefreq>
 <priority>0.80</priority>
</url>
<url>
 <loc>http://qnimate.com/category/web-development/</loc>
 <changefreq>weekly</changefreq>
 <priority>0.80</priority>
</url>
</urlset>
```

I have named this XML file as sitemap.xml and placed it in website's root directory.

Here I provide list of all webpages of my websites and also their priority and content change frequency.

There is no guarantee that search engines will crawl all the webpages listed in sitemap.

There are many online tools to generate sitemap for your website. My favorite is XML Sitemap Generator(http://www.xml-sitemaps.com/).

To learn more about sitemaps visit Google's official documentation on Sitemaps(https://support.google.com/webmasters/topic/4581713?hl=en&ref_topic=4589290).

Robot Exclusion Protocol

Robots exclusion protocol provides us the ability to instruct search engines about what parts of the website should be crawled and what shouldn't be crawled.

These instructions can be provided using robots meta tag, robots HTTP headers or robots text file. I prefer to provide this instructions via robots text file.

You can place all the instructions in a file named robots.txt and place it in website's root directory.

This is an example of robots.txt file:

```
User-agent: googlebot
Disallow: /about/privacy
Disallow: /full_data_use_policy
Disallow: /legal/terms
Disallow: /policy.php

User-agent: *
Disallow: /
```

Here we are not allowing Google crawler to crawl some privacy and terms pages. But allowing it to crawl all other webpages in our website. And we are not allowing any other search engine to crawl anything.

You can find complete reference on Robots exclusion protocol at http://www.robotstxt.org/.

Page Speed

Webpages which load faster have more chances of getting higher in search result. Google recommends webpage load time to be less than equal to 5 seconds. If your website is talking more than average time then you are missing one of the most important SEO factors. There are several ways to increase page load time.

Web Caching

Web caching is defined as storing HTTP responses locally by web browser so that the resources doesn't have to be loaded every time its requested.

Web caching makes browsing faster and saves a lot of bandwidth. Search engines look for web caching HTTP headers in HTTP responses. Therefore if your website is responding with web caching headers then your website is given a better authority.

I have explained technical details about web caching in a complete separate chapter.

This is the code you can put into your .htaccess file if you are using apache web server.

```
<IfModule mod_expires.c>
ExpiresActive On
ExpiresByType image/jpg "access 1 year"
ExpiresByType image/jpeg "access 1 year"
ExpiresByType image/gif "access 1 year"
ExpiresByType image/png "access 1 year"
ExpiresByType text/css "access 1 month"
ExpiresByType text/html "access 1 month"
ExpiresByType application/pdf "access 1 month"
ExpiresByType text/x-javascript "access 1 month"
ExpiresByType application/x-shockwave-flash "access 1 month"
ExpiresByType image/x-icon "access 1 year"
ExpiresDefault "access 1 month"
</IfModule>
```

Here we are instructing the browser to cache the most common static resources. Therefore these files are not needed to be download again and again.

Code Minification

Removing unnecessary characters from source code decreases the file size and also decrease file downloading time. Minifying CSS, HTML and JavaScript code will help to increase webpage loading speed.

There are many online tools available for minifying your code. My favorite is YUI compressor(http://refresh-sf.com/yui/). Its a free tool and is very easy to use.

Compressing

Compressing HTTP responses with gzip or deflate will decrease resources downloading time. Gzip or deflate should be only used if browser can decompress the compressed resources. While making a request, browser explicitly tell about their compressing and decompressing ability.

This is the code you can put in your .htaccess file if your are using apache web server.

```
AddOutputFilterByType DEFLATE text/plain
AddOutputFilterByType DEFLATE text/html
AddOutputFilterByType DEFLATE text/xml
AddOutputFilterByType DEFLATE text/css
AddOutputFilterByType DEFLATE application/xml
AddOutputFilterByType DEFLATE application/xhtml+xml
AddOutputFilterByType DEFLATE application/rss+xml
AddOutputFilterByType DEFLATE application/javascript
AddOutputFilterByType DEFLATE application/x-javascript
```

Here we are compressing resources like text, HTML, XML, CSS and JavaScript.

Now the size of these resource are decreased and therefore loading time also decreases.

Redirection and Duplicate content

In this chapter we will see the different ways to redirect URL's and how those techniques will effect our website's search engine ranking. We will also have a look at the different ways of handling duplicate content in our websites and how search engines handle duplicate content if we don't specify anything. Having a good knowledge on redirection and duplicate content handling will help you to optimize your website for search engine ranking.

URL Redirection

URL redirection is sending users and search engines to another URL from the one they originally requested.

URL redirection is done due to the following reasons:

- Website has been moved to new domain: Suppose qscutter.com is now moved to plus.qscutter.com. Then we need to redirect all users requesting qscutter.com to plus.qscutter.com

- Multiple domain names: qnimate.com and www.qnimate.com point to the same website so we need to redirect all requests to qnimate.com

- Shortening: Sometimes we need to create short URLs for our long ones because of word limits in blogs, comments and other platforms. For example qnimate.com/this-is-my-category/this-is-my-page/ can be shortened to qnimate.com/?page=1. And when user visits qnimate.com/?page=1, the qnimate web server will redirect user to qnimate.com/this-is-my-category/this-is-my-page.

- Handling duplicate content: redirection is also used to discard multiple pages and URLs having same content. This chapter explains more on handling duplicate content using redirection. We will get in depth into this topic.

What are the different types of redirection?

There are many ways to redirect URLs. All these methods are categorised into two categories, HTTP redirection and HTML redirection.

HTTP Redirection

Redirection done using HTTP Location header and HTTP status code 3XX is called HTTP Redirection. There are many types of HTTP redirection.

- 300 Redirect or Multiple Choices
- 301 Redirect or permanent redirect
- 302 Redirect or Found or Temporary Redirect
- 303 Redirect or See Other
- 307 Redirect or Temporary Redirect
- 308 Redirect or Permanent Redirect
- HTTP refresh header

Remember that all HTTP status code beginning with 3 are not redirects. For example 304, 305 and 306 status codes are not redirects.

HTML Redirection

Redirection done using HTML and Javascript code called HTML redirection. Browsers recognise HTML redirection.

There are mainly two types of HTML redirection
- Refresh Meta Tag
- JavaScript redirects

Search engines don't execute HTML code, they just parse it. Therefore search engine will not recognize Javascript redirects. Search engines always parse meta tags, so search engines will know about the refresh meta tags.

301 Redirect or permanent redirect

This is used when we completely move our web pages to new domain or new URL. Search engines will never visit this URL again instead directly visit the URL specified in the Location header.

Note that when we use 301 redirect, the redirection request is made GET regardless of the original request.

302 Redirect or Found or Temporary Redirect

This is used when we have temporarily moved our web pages to new domain or new URL. Search engines will index the new URLs temporarily and disable the original URLs. Search engine in this case will crawl both original and temporary URLs at constant interval. Once it finds the original URLs not redirecting anymore, then they will enable the original ones in the index and remove the temporary URLs from index.

Note that if a web page temporarily redirects for more than few days than the rank of the page in search result will start going down. That means keeping a website down for long time will decease its ranking in search engine result.

In HTTP 1.0 its called as Found and in HTTP 1.1 its called as Temporary Redirect.

All HTTP clients don't implement 302 redirect in the same way. Some clients make the redirection request type to be same as original request type. While some clients make the redirection request type to be GET regardless of the original request type.

HTTP 303 Redirect and 307 Redirect

303 and 307 are also used for temporary redirection of URLs. 303 and 307 are recognized by HTTP 1.1 clients only.

302 redirect implementation differs according to client. So 303 and 307 were introduced for proper implementation.

When we send 303 status code, we are explicitly asking the client to make the redirect request as GET regardless of the type of original request.

the sources from where your users come from and how long they stay, for that you can pass GET parameters to the URL and monitor the time using AJAX. For example: qnimate.com/index.html?src=facebook. For search engine it seems like qnimate.com/index.html and qnimate.com/index.html?src=facebook are two different URL. It also sees that they both generate same content so they consider these URLs to have duplicate content. These two URLs now have different search ranking.

• Multiple URLs: A page can have different URLs. qnimate.com/24-august displays the post published on 24th august. And qnimate.com/24-august/18:00 displays the post published on 18:00 in the same date. And it is possible that these two URLs generate the same page.

• Domain names: www.qnimate.com and qnimate.com point to the same webpage. But search engines take them as two different URLs, which causes duplicate content.

Problems caused due to duplicate content

• Search engines don't know which page to be displayed in search result.

- Search engines don't know whether to pass all pagerank to one URL or divide among all those URLs.

Solution to duplicate content?

There are basically three solutions for handling duplicate content.

- Canonical link element
- Redirection
- Robots meta tag or X-Robots-Tag HTTP header field or robots.txt

Canonical link element as an solution to duplicate content

Let's learn canonical link element implementation with an example.

Suppose qnimate.com/index.html is the home page. If you want to monitor the sources from where your users come from and how long they stay, for that you can pass GET parameters to the URL and monitor the time using AJAX. For example: qnimate.com/index.html?src=facebook. For search engine it seems like qnimate.com/index.html and qnimate.com/index.html?src=facebook are two different URL. It also sees that they both generate same content so they consider these URLs to have duplicate content. These two URLs now have different search ranking.

We can use rel=canonical meta tag to instruct search engine that they both are same and all ranking power of qnimate.com/index.html?src=facebook should be passed to qnimate.com/index.html.

Let's the the code implementation:

qnimate.com/index.html

```
<!doctype html>
<html>
<head>
<title>A programming blog</title>
</head>
<body>
body content!!!!
</body>
</html>
```

qnimate.com/index.html?src=facebook

```
<!doctype html>
<html>
<head>
<title>A programming blog</title>
<link href="http://qnimate.com" rel="canonical" />
</head>
<body>
body content!!!!
</body>
</html>
```

When search engine will visit the second URL it will encounter rel=canonical meta tag so it will pass all ranking power of this URL to the first one. And also search engine will display first URL in search result.

HTTP Redirection as an solution to duplicate content

Permanent redirection passes all ranking power of original URL to the redirect URL. But temporary redirection doesn't pass any ranking power.

Let's look at an example of using HTTP permanent redirection.

http://www.qnimate.com and http://qnimate.com are two different URLs pointing to same web page. So we can redirect all requests from http://www.qnimate.com to http://qnimate.com permanently.

For example:

http://www.qnimate.com

```
<?php
    header('HTTP/1.1 301 Moved Temporarily');
    header('Location: http://qnimate.com/');
    exit();
?>
```

Robots meta tag as an solution to duplicate content

By using robots meta tag we can instruct the search engine to not crawl specific pages or to crawl specific pages. Using robots meta tag we cannot pass ranking power of one page to another.

Let's take an example:

Suppose we have two pages with same content. Let those pages be http://qnimate.com/1.html and http://qnimate.com/2.html. We want search engine to index and display only http://qnimate.com/1.html and ignore http://qnimate.com/2.html. So we can add robots meta tag in http://qnimate.com/2.html and instruct the search engine to ignore it.

http://qnimate.com/2.html

```
<html>
<head>
<meta name="robots" content="noindex">
</head>
</html>
```

This same thing can be achieved using X-Robots-Tag HTTP header field and robots.txt file.

Web Caching

One of the ways by which you can make your websites faster is by using web caching techniques. There are a lot of confusions related to web caching. Develops usually get confused about how web caching information is understood by proxies, browser and crawlers. In this chapter I will give all details about web caching.

If you not a web developer, you are just reading this book to optimise your website for search ranking than you can skip this chapter.

What is Web Caching?

Caching is storing something temporarily for fast retrieval later on.

Web Caching is storing of HTTP responses temporarily for fast retrieval later on.

Advantage of web caching

Web caching reduces the number of requests made to the server. Due to which less bandwidth is consumed and web server load is reduced. It also helps users to visit a web page if web server is down.

Systems using web caching

Search Engines, Web Browsers, Content Delivery Networks and Web Proxies are some systems which widely cache web files. Systems have their different purpose of web caching.

Web caching in CDNs, proxies and web browsers

The caching mechanism of these systems can be controlled using caching meta tags or HTTP caching headers. These systems do caching to decrease the bandwidth usage and also decrease web server overload.

We can control the caching behavior using Last-Modified/If-Modified-Since, ETag/If-None-Match, Cache-Control and Expires headers(or meta tags). Cache-Control was introduced in HTTP 1.1 whereas Expires header has introduced in HTTP 1.0. So we must use both of them for better support of clients. Similarly Last-Modified/If-Modified-Since was introduced in HTTP 1.0 but ETag/If-None-Match was introduced in

HTTP 1.1. So we can rely on using Last-Modified/If-Modified-Since.

Cache-Control header is used to instruct these systems how to cache the response. It is responsible for controlling the freshness. It can have eight possible values. These values are:

• public: The web page can be cached by any cache and can be served to any user.

• private: Caches on these systems can be shared among many users or a single user. When a cache is made for a single user then we call it as a non-shared cache. If the cache is made for all users than we call it as shared cache. private indicates that only cache the response if it is stored in non-shared cache.

• no-cache: systems will cache the response. But before serving these systems send a If-Modified-Since header(assigned to the date same as Last-Modified) GET request for confirmation to server. If server responds 304 than cached version is served otherwise if 200 response is sent by server than the currently received response is served and old response is removed from cache. If-Modified-Since header is only sent if Last-Modified header was sent by server during cache-control response. If Last-Modified header is send by the server then client will do revalidation of the cache using If-Modified-Since otherwise client will revalidate without Last-Modified-Since header due to which server will have no way to identify its a validation request and so it will always respond with 200 status which will cause refetching. we can use ETag/If-None-Match instead of Last-Modified/If-Modified-Since.

- no-store: Systems do not cache the response at all.

- max-age: Specifies in seconds the amount of time the response will be cached. After the response has expired its deleted from the cache.

- s-maxage: same as max-age but for proxy servers

- must-revalidate: Specifies that no matter what the condition is before serving cached content to user the system must send a If-Modified-Since request to the server for confirmation. If-Modified-Since header is only sent if Last-Modified header was sent by server during cache-control response. If Last-Modified header is send by the server then client will do revalidation of the cache using If-Modified-Since otherwise client will revalidate without Last-Modified-Since header due to which server will have no way to identify its a validation request and so it will always respond with 200 status which will cause refetching. we can use ETag/If-None-Match instead of Last-Modified/If-Modified-Since.

- proxy-revalidate: Same as must-revalidate but for proxy servers.

- pre-check and post-check: These values are supported by IE only. They provide better control over expiry time than max-age. I skipped these two headers because they are not supported in other browsers so its not important to learn about them. If you still want to learn about them then visit http://blogs.msdn.com/b/ieinternals/archive/2009/07/20/using-post_2d00_check-and-pre_2d00_check-cache-directives.aspx.

Expires header can also be used to instruct these systems how to cache response. If Expires header is assigned an future date and time then the response is cache till that time and requests are not made to the server. But if it is assigned to a past time or -1 then these systems do not cache the response. Expires header has no way to instruct client to revalidate cache. Even if we provide Expires header with Last-Modified the client will not revalidate the cache.

Let's see some examples of using these headers:

```
Expires: -1
Cache-Control: no-store
```

or

```
<meta http-equiv="Expires" content="-1" />
<meta http-equiv="Cache-Control" content="no-store" />
```

Here these systems will not cache the response.

```
Expires: Thu, 15 Aug 2060 09:00:00 GMT
Cache-Control: no-cache, must-revalidate, expires=360000000
```

Here these systems will cache the response but before serving the response the client will try to revalidate but as we didn't provide Last-Modified header, client will send revalidation request without If-Modified-Since and therefore server will response with 200 status code which is refetching the page again.

```
Expires: Thu, 15 Aug 2015 09:00:00 GMT
Last-Modified: Thu, 15 Aug 2011 09:00:00 GMT
```

Here browser will cache the document till 15 Aug 2015 09:00:00. Client will not revalidate the cache before serving.

If the cached document expires then its re-fetched or re-validated. Its re-validated if Last-Modified or E-tag header was provided by the server while the response was stored in cache. So if Last-Modified (assigned to the date when response was last modified) is present then client sends a If-Modified-Since header to confirm weather the cached copy is still valid or not. If server responds with 304 then client continuous using the cached copy after it has expired. If the server responds with 200 status code then the cached copy is removed and the new response is served to the user. Same way it works for E-Tag. E-Tag is a calculated hash of the response content. Server uses it to check if the document is modified or not. And responds accordingly. More on calculation of E-tag visit http://en.wikipedia.org/wiki/HTTP_ETag. If none of these Last-Modified and E-Tag is provided while caching the document then after cache expires the client re-fetches the while document.

Let's see an example to make it clear how Last-Modified and E-Tag works. Suppose we have 2 files one.js and two.js.

one.js HTTP response

```
Last-Modified: Thu, 11 Feb 2011 10:00:00 GMT
Expires: Thu, 15 Aug 2060 09:00:00 GMT
Cache-Control: public, must-revalidate, expires=360000000
```

two.js HTTP response

```
Expires: Thu, 15 Aug 2060 09:00:00 GMT
Cache-Control: public, expires=360000000
```

In two.js we did not provided the Last-Modified header while caching it. So once it expires in 2060 the client will download the file again instead of re-validating using If-Modified-Since. But for one.js the client will verify using the If-Modified-Since header during every request and also after cache expires. If server responds 304 then client continuous using the cached copy.

Sometimes web servers also cache requests. So that they don't have to read the same files from the disk again and again. Sometimes browsers, CDNs or proxies don't like it. They may need fresh server execution for the request, so they can use Pragma HTTP request header to ask for fresh response.

How is expiration time calculated

expirationTime = responseTime + freshnessLifetime – currentAge

The freshness lifetime is calculated based on several headers. If a "Cache-control: max-age=N" header is specified, then the freshness lifetime is equal to N. If this header is not present, which is very often the case, then we look for an"Expires" header. If an "Expires" header exists, then its value minus the value of the "Date" header determines the freshness lifetime. Finally, if neither header is present, then we look for a "Last-Modified" header. If this header is present, then the cache's freshness lifetime is equal to the value of the "Date" header minus the value of the "Last-modified" header divided by 10. If none of this headers are there then the response is not cached.

responseTime is the time at which the response was received according to the client.

The current age is usually close to zero, but is influenced by the presence of an Age header, which proxy caches may add to indicate the length of time a document has been sitting in its cache. The precise algorithm, which attempts avoid error resulting from clock skew, is described in RFC 2616 section 13.2.3(http://tools.ietf.org/html/rfc2616#section-13.2.3).

Web caching in search engines

Search engines do caching so that if the website is down than they can provide the cached version of the web page to the user. This caching is done by a search engine component called as indexer. In Google search result you can see a link to cached version of every web page.

We can avoid search engines from displaying cached version of a web page by the following ways:

robots.txt

```
User-agent: *
Noarchive: /
```

or

Meta Tag

```
<meta name="robots" content="noarchive" />
```

or

HTTP Response header

```
X-Robots-Tag: noarchive
```

Search engine crawlers (a component of search engine responsible for downloading pages) don't do caching. They decide revisits to web pages by using some complicated algorithms. But still there is a way we can force the crawlers to cache pages they visit so that they don't download the same content again and again.

We can control search engines from downloading the same content or page again and again by using Last-Modified/If-Modified-Since or ETag/If-None-Match headers.

Example of using Last-Modified/If-Modified-Since:

When a request is made by search engine the server returns HTTP response with Last-Modified header. This header indicates when the file was last modified.

```
Last-Modified: Mon, 15 August 2003 00:00:00 GMT
```

Now when search engine revisits the same file it puts If-Modified-Since header in HTTP request.

```
If-Modified-Since: Mon, 15 August 2003 00:00:00 GMT
```

Now the server sees the If-Modified-Since header and checks if it was modified since then or not. If its modified than it returns a normal 200 success response. And can include Last-Modified header if needed again. But if its not modified than server returns 304 Page Not Modified response. On return of 304 response, search engines consider the previously indexed information to be still fresh and valid.

In this way we can control the caching behavior of both components crawler and indexer. Remember that these techniques has no effect on the crawler revisit policy and priority on a web page.

Pagination

Pagination is one of the most important aspects of SEO. E-Commerce websites and Blogs needs to take care of pagination. A bad way of handling pagination could cause penalty to your website by search engines. In this chapter I will talk all about pagination.

What Is Pagination And What Are Its SEO Impacts?

Pagination is when your divide a webpage into multiple pages. Mostly Blogs and E-Commerce websites do pagination. Blogs and E-Commerce do pagination so that they can decrease the page loading time of the page and can decrease server load.

This is a simple example of pagination

page1.html	page2.html	page3.html	profile123.html
Hello, I Am Narayan	I Am A Web And Mobile Developer	I Love Blogging. It Helps Me to Learn More	Hello, I am Narayan. I Am A Web And Mobile Developer. I Love Blogging. It Helps Me To Learn More

Here I have written about me in three different pages and linking them using hyperlinks(next and prev anchor links). And I also have a page where complete profile is found. This complete profile page in SEO terms is called as "View All" page. "View All" page is slower due to lot of text but other three pages load fast.

But search engines don't know anything about this. They will index these four pages differently and send users to different pages according the search. If someone reads about me in second page then the user will not know my name, this is the problem of pagination. I have to figure out a way to force all users to land on my first page or "View All" page.

Another problem is that these four pages will have different page rankings which is not what we want. There are the same and should have same ranking.

Solving Pagination Problems

Search Engines never ask you to stop using Pagination rather they want websites to guide them while crawling and indexing paginated pages.

The solutions to pagination problems is shown in the below image

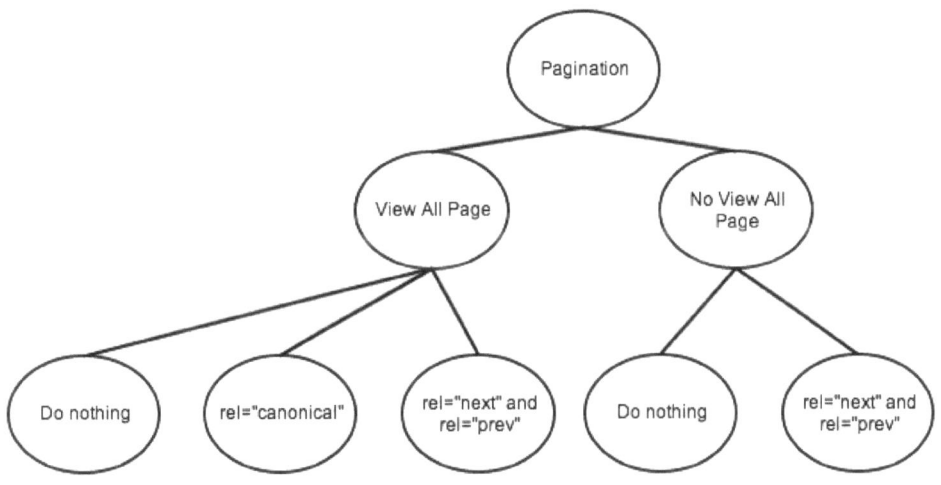

We can see that solution completely depends on weather we are using the "View All" page or not.

Let's see these solutions in depth.

Doing Nothing

This solution works for both situations(having view all page or not). You can leave the pagination as it is.

"View All" Page

Search engines are equipped with enough artificial intelligence that they can find "view all" page if present and show only "view all" page in the search result. They can detect the paginated content by analyzing HTML markup and duplicate content. But search engines will not pass ranking factors of paginated pages to "View All" page.

No "View All" Page

If you don't have a "View All" page they also you can leave it as it is, search engines will try to identify pagination and show only first page in search result. First page will be shown for queries matching other paginated pages. But search engines will not pass ranking factors of paginated pages to the first page in pagination.

In either case("view All" page is there or not) search engines will crawl and index all the paginated pages.

But doing nothing about it is always a risk because all search engines are not smart enough.

Canonical Link As A Solution

We have talked about canonical link in redirection and duplicate content chapter.

Canonical link element is actually used to handle duplicate content in web pages. But having a "View All" page is also like having duplicate content and therefore we can use canonical link to force search engines to crawl and index only "View All" page and display on search result.

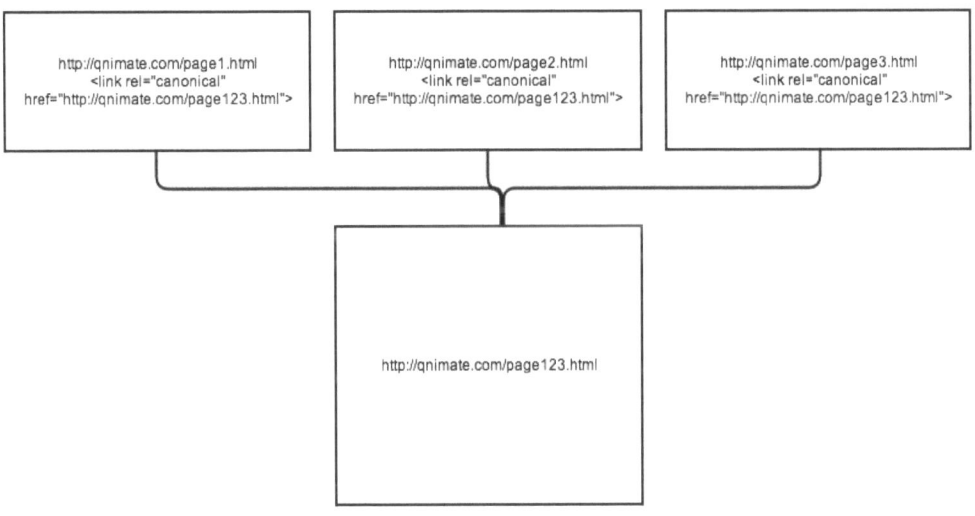

"View All" duplicates content of the paginated pages and so we can use canonical link element to solve the problem of pagination. But if there is no "View All" page then there is no duplicate content and so we cannot use canonical link element.

Using Canonical link element we can pass all the ranking of paginated page to "View All" page. Search engines will now only index the "View All" page and discard the paginated pages.

Next And Previous Link Elements

Next and Previous link elements are the best way to solve the pagination problems.

```
http://qnimate.com/page1.html          http://qnimate.com/page2.html          http://qnimate.com/page3.html
     <link rel="next"                       <link rel="prev"                       <link rel="prev"
href="http://qnimate.com/page2.html">  href="http://qnimate.com/page1.html">  href="http://qnimate.com/page2.html">
                                            <link rel="next"
                                       href="http://qnimate.com/page3.html">
```

Use of next and previous link elements is independent of "View All" page. So you can use next and previous link elements if you have or don't have next and previous link elements.

Next and previous link elements pass all ranking factors of paginated pages to the first paginated page. Search engines will crawl and index all pages but only show the first page. First page will be shown for queries matching other paginated pages.

Although you have a "View All" page, search engines will display the first paginated page.

Canonical Link To First Page

You must be having a question in mind, "Why cannot we use canonical link to point to first page when view all page is not present?".

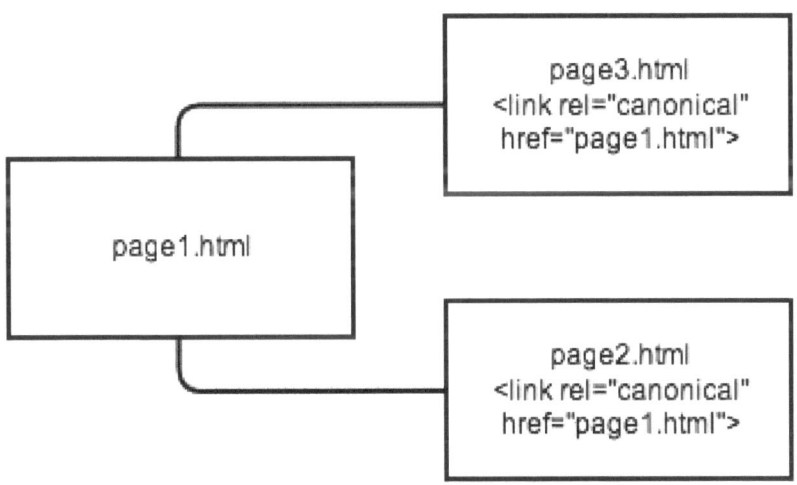

The answer is when we use canonical link, search engines will index only the target page not the source pages. Therefore queries matching source pages will never be matched in search result and so first page will not appear for queries related to other paginated pages.

Authorship

You might have seen people's faces appearing on Google search results. Specifically when the content of those links belong to a particular author. Have you have ever wondered how they do that? There are basically two ways of doing this. In this chapter we will look at both the ways.

Our objective is to get similar Google search results

QNimate
qnimate.com/
by Narayan Prusty
QNimate is a blog maintained by Narayan Prusty. Posts are mostly focused on programming.

What is Google Authorship?

Linking web page content to Google+ profile is called as Google Authorship.

Remember that Google Authorship is applied to web pages. So a website can have multiple authors linking to their Google+ profiles.

Google Authorship - Method One

You can make the author's picture to be displayed on Google search result by simply adding the below code snippet to your web page and then linking to your website from your Google+ profile.

    <a href="https://plus.google.com/[-author-profile-id-]?rel=author">Narayan</a>

Here you need to remember two things. First replace the [-author-profile-id-] with the real id of the author. Second don't forget to insert the query string ?rel=author. You can put this code snippet anywhere in your web page.

To get your Google+ Profile Id, you need to visit your Google+ profile page and then on the Web Address bar you will be able to see a large random number like "104311688576740431059" in the URL. That's your Profile Id

Now you need to visit your Google+ profile page and add your website URL as a contributor link. To do this visit http://plus.google.com/me/about/edit/co and now click on "Add custom link" to add your website url. Now you are done.

Google Authorship - Method Two

You can also submit necessary information to Google so that Google will display your picture in search result.

You need to have the following things setup before going for this method:

- Make sure that you have a Google+ profile photo with a recognisable headshot.
- . Make sure that a byline containing your name appears on each page of your content (for example, "By Narayan Prusty").
- Make sure that you have a email address in the same domain as your content. (ex: abc@yourdomain.com)

Once you have the following things are setup you can visit https://plus.google.com/authorship to submit your information to Google.

For multiple authors you have to do this steps multiple times.

SEO impact of Authorship

Webpages with verified authors get a better page authority and therefore has more chances to get listed higher in search result. It is very much recommended for blogs and other kinds of content rich websites.

10

National And Local SEO

If you website provides service to people in a particular location or country then Local SEO, National SEO and On-Site Optimizations will help your website rank well in local search queries.

What is Local Search?

Local search are those searches which are constrained to a particular geographic location. In simple words we can say local search is when we search for something at a particular place or location.

Searching for restaurants at Bangalore or searching for tourist places in India. These both are referring to a particular location.

Local search can be implicit or explicit. Lets discuss them in details:

Local search is explicit when we mention the location and service. For example, "hospitals in bangalore" is treated to be explicit local search.

Local search is implicit when we mention the service only. For example, "gyms" is treated to be implicit search. Searches engines have the ability to identify search queries which are typically consumed locally. Here search engine identify the word "gyms" to be a local service and then they provide information about nearby gyms. When we make a implicit search, search engines use our IP address and search engine TLD(google.co.in, google.co.uk etc) to identify our country and location.

On-Site Optimization

Whenever users make a local search, search engines look for matching webpages with location keywords and service keywords. Having location specific keywords and service keywords in your webpages is called on-site optimization.

For example, if you have a website for your restaurant which is located in Bangalore, India. Suppose a user explicitly searches for "restaurants in bangalore", then search engines look for the words "restaurants" and "bangalore" in your website. Therefore you need to have location and service keywords in your website. If a user from Bangalore would have implicitly searched for "restaurants" then search engines will change the query to "restaurants in bangalore" and then processed the query.

On-Site Optimization can be done using Postal Address Structured Data(http://schema.org/PostalAddress). And also by specifying country and/or city name in title, description and page content. Google will automatically parse and understand to which country and/or city you website provides services to.

National SEO

We saw how we can use On-Site optimizations to provide search engines about our location. But we can also explicitly provide location of our business. National And Local SEO helps us to provide details of our service and location to search engines explicitly.

National SEO is used to provide the country to which you provide services. Therefore people looking for services in that specific country will see your website.

You can signal search engines the country to which you provide services to by using the country specific TLD(.co.in, .co.kr, .co.uk etc). If you want to use non-country specific TLD(.com, .edu etc) and still want to tell search engines about your service country then use

Google webmaster tools to specify the country. Visit https://www.google.com/webmasters/tools/settings and select country in Geographic target.

When you use country specific TLD, search engines only display your website in country specific search engines(i.e, qnimate.co.in will be displayed in google.co.in not in google.co.kr) for implicit search queries. But if user explicitly searches for it then search engines display our website in other TLD search engines.

Local SEO

Using Local SEO you can provide exact location of your business.

For Local SEO you need to create a Business page in Google+ and go through extra validation steps. Local SEO will also add your office location to Google Maps. So if your website matches a search query(On-Site optimization) then along with your website name, your physical location will be shown in the search result.

For complete steps on Local SEO visit https://support.google.com/plus/answer/1713911.

11

Multi-language SEO and Multi-currency SEO

Building a multi-language website is not a difficult task. But making it search friendly is a tricky task. In this chapter I will provide all possible ways to make your multi-language website search friendly.

What is a Multi-language and Multi-currency website?

A multi-language website is a website which have different language versions of webpages. This is done for making website more user friendly to people who speak different languages.

Mostly International new channels, social networking sites etc have multiple language versions of their website.

Similarly multi-currency website is a website which have different currency versions of their website.

Mostly E-commerce websites are multi-currency websites.

URL Structure For Multi-language/Multi-currency website?

Multi-language/Multi-currency website can be achieved by using any of the following URL structures:

Subdirectory

By creating different sub-directories.
For example: qnimate.com/us/apple-buys-beats/, qnimate.com/in/apple-buys-beats/, qnimate.com/kr/apple-buys-beats/, qnimate.com/apple-buys-beats/

Subdomains

By creating different sub-domains of the website.
For example: us.qnimate.com/apple-buys-beats/, in.qnimate.com/apple-buys-beats/, kr.qnimate.com/apple-buys-beats/, qnimate.com/apple-buys-beats/

TLDs

By creating different Top Level Domains of the website.

For example: qnimate.co.us/apple-buys-beats/, qnimate.co.in/apple-buys-beats/, qnimate.co.kr/apple-buys-beats/, qnimate.com/apple-buys-beats/

Different Domains

By creating different domains of the website.
For example: qnimateus.com/apple-buys-beats/, qnimateindia/apple-buys-beats/, qnimatekorean/apple-buys-beats/, qnimate.com/apple-buys-beats.

Search Problems In Multi-language/ Multi-currency Websites

There are few problems search engines face while crawling, indexing and displaying search result of multi-language or multi-currency websites.

Identifying Language Variations

Suppose you have a news item in two different languages. And the urls are qnimate.com/us/apple-buys-beats/ and qnimate.com/uk/apple-buys-beats/. The first URL is for US users and then second URL is for UK users. But search engines don't know this language variation you have implemented. Therefore search engines display any one page from these two in search result(search engines choose one from these two using page ranking factors but not by language factor). So there is chances that someone using google.co.uk will get qnimate.com/us/apple-buys-beats/ in search result instead of qnimate.com/uk/apple-buys-beats/.

Ranking Factors Of Pages

Let's consider the same example as we considered above. As search engines don't know that these two pages content same content in different languages, search engines will assign different search ranking to these two pages. But actually both should have same search ranking.

rel="alternate" As A Solution To Search Problems

The above problems can be solved using rel="alternate".

Suppose we have five URLs with same content in different language or currency. Then we can apply rel="alternate" this way:

us.qnimate.com/apple-buys-beats/

```html
<head>
   <title>QNimate - Apple Buys Beats - United States</title>
   <link rel="alternate" href="http://us.qnimate.com/apple-buys-beats" hreflang="en-us" />
   <link rel="alternate" href="http://au.qnimate.com/apple-buys-beats" hreflang="en-au" />
   <link rel="alternate" href="http://en.qnimate.com/apple-buys-beats" hreflang="en" />
   <link rel="alternate" href="http://es.qnimate.com/apple-buys-beats" hreflang="es" />
   <link rel="alternate" href="http://qnimate.com/apple-buys-beats/" hreflang="x-default" />
<head>
```

au.qnimate.com/apple-buys-beats/

```html
<head>
   <title>QNimate - Apple Buys Beats - Australia</title>
   <link rel="alternate" href="http://us.qnimate.com/apple-buys-beats" hreflang="en-us" />
   <link rel="alternate" href="http://au.qnimate.com/apple-buys-beats" hreflang="en-au" />
   <link rel="alternate" href="http://en.qnimate.com/apple-buys-beats" hreflang="en" />
   <link rel="alternate" href="http://es.qnimate.com/apple-buys-beats" hreflang="es" />
   <link rel="alternate" href="http://qnimate.com/apple-buys-beats/" hreflang="x-default" />
<head>
```

en.qnimate.com/apple-buys-beats/

```html
<head>
   <title>QNimate - Apple Buys Beats - English</title>
   <link rel="alternate" href="http://us.qnimate.com/apple-buys-beats" hreflang="en-us" />
   <link rel="alternate" href="http://au.qnimate.com/apple-buys-beats" hreflang="en-au" />
   <link rel="alternate" href="http://en.qnimate.com/apple-buys-beats" hreflang="en" />
   <link rel="alternate" href="http://es.qnimate.com/apple-buys-beats" hreflang="es" />
   <link rel="alternate" href="http://qnimate.com/apple-buys-beats/" hreflang="x-default" />
<head>
```

es.qnimate.com/apple-buys-beats/

```
<head>
    <title>QNimate - Apple Buys Beats - Spanish</title>
    <link rel="alternate" href="http://us.qnimate.com/apple-buys-beats" hreflang="en-us" />
    <link rel="alternate" href="http://au.qnimate.com/apple-buys-beats" hreflang="en-au" />
    <link rel="alternate" href="http://en.qnimate.com/apple-buys-beats" hreflang="en" />
    <link rel="alternate" href="http://es.qnimate.com/apple-buys-beats" hreflang="es" />
    <link rel="alternate" href="http://qnimate.com/apple-buys-beats/" hreflang="x-default" />
<head>
```

qnimate.com/apple-buys-beats/

```
<head>
    <title>QNimate - Apple Buys Beats</title>
    <link rel="alternate" href="http://us.qnimate.com/apple-buys-beats" hreflang="en-us" />
    <link rel="alternate" href="http://au.qnimate.com/apple-buys-beats" hreflang="en-au" />
    <link rel="alternate" href="http://en.qnimate.com/apple-buys-beats" hreflang="en" />
    <link rel="alternate" href="http://es.qnimate.com/apple-buys-beats" hreflang="es" />
    <link rel="alternate" href="http://qnimate.com/apple-buys-beats/" hreflang="x-default" />
<head>
```

We have to provide all alternate links in all the multi variation pages of the same conent. This avoids outsiders claiming your webpages to be verions of their pages.

Now all the above links will have same search ranking power.

Search engine first finds the pages with matching words as the search query. Then filters using the google search language. And returns a single URL which is the best match.

Suppose a user using google.co.uk searches for "qnimate apple buys beats", then all the five pages match the query. But only http://en.qnimate.com/apple-buys-beats is displayed as this is the english version of the page for english users apart from Australia and USA. If the same user searches for "qnimate apple buys beats spanish" then only http://es.qnimate.com/apple-buys-beats matches the search query and therefore google returns this page.

If a user using google.fr searches for "qnimate apple buys beats", then all five pages match the search query. But as the user is using french version of google, google looks for french version of the pages. But doesn't find a french version so returns http://qnimate.com/apple-buys-beats/ which is the default page. If the query is changed to "qnimate apple buys beats french" then no page matchs all the query words. Therefore none of the URLs will be listed in the search result.

How Is Multi-language SEO Different From National/Local SEO?

Local/National SEO is used to target users based on location but Multi-language SEO targets users based on language.

For example, While using Local/National SEO the searches made using google.com/?hl=bn, google.com/?hl=hi or google.com/?hl=mr are treated to be same. But for language SEO these three google searches represent different set of people.

12

Pagerank

Pagerank is a algorithm that made Google the leader of search engines. In this chapter we will discuss in depth about pagerank and how it affects SEO. Pagerank is off-page SEO factor.

What is pagerank?

When search engines were first developed, they ranked all webpage equally and would return results based only on the content and meta tags the pages contained. At the time, however, the PageRank system would revolutionize search engine rankings by including one key factor: a webpage authority.

PageRank is a numeric value that represents how important a page is on the web. Google figures that when one page links to another page, it is effectively casting a vote for the other page. The more votes that are cast for a page, the more important the page must be.

Building backlinks

Building backlinks to webpages in your website will help webpages of your website get better authority and therefore rank better in search results.

Remember that the webpages linking to your webpages must be of same category and relevant. Otherwise webpages providing spammy backlinks will loose pagerank. Search engines use very complex algorithms to find spams in the web.

Purchasing backlinks is consider black hat SEO and the webpages which sells links will have a pagerank penalty. Good pagerank depends on quality of backlinks not the number of backlinks.

Here are some white hat ways to build backlinks:

- Make sure you have great content in your website. So that others will automatically link to your website.
- Make sure your website provide RSS feed. People who subscribe to your RSS feed provide attribution links to your website.
- Start linking to other relevant sites therefore they will also start linking to you.
- Writing guest posts will also help to build back links.

- Make a news release about your website. News sites often link to website on the news page.
- Write reviews about different products on other websites. There is a good chance that they will link to your website.
- Be very active on social networking sites. Its a great way to build backlinks.
- Get yourself interviewed. People will start linking to your websites if they like your interview.
- Provide affiliation if your website is a E-commerce website. This is a good way to build backlinks.

There are many other ways to build relevant backlinks. As more and more you get into Internet marketing you will find new ways.

nofollow

Google implemented a new value, "nofollow", for the rel attribute of HTML link and anchor elements, so that website developers can make links that Google will not consider for the purposes of PageRank—they are links that no longer constitute a "vote" in the PageRank system. The nofollow relationship was added in an attempt to help combat spamdexing.

You must use nofollow links in your websites areas like comments, reviews etc. Therefore people will not comments to get backlinks.

Markup for nofollow looks like this:

<a href="http://qnimate.com" rel="nofollow">QNimate</a>

13

Miscellaneous

In this chapters we will discuss many frequently asked questions, confusions and common mistakes done by website owners.

Using Deprecated Tags

Its not a good idea to use deprecated tags. For search engines it seems like your website is poorly maintained and content is not updated. Therefore there is chances of doing bad in SEO.

Responsive Website

Responsive websites get a chance to rank higher in mobile search. Mobile users look for responsive sites so that content is readable and navigation is easy. Prefer to make your website responsive.

Use of underscores as separators

Many people use underscores in URLs and other places as separators. But search engines don't consider underscores as separators. Use dash or comma as separators.

Flash content in websites

Try to make your website independent of flash content. Flash is not supported by many mobile and desktop browsers. Therefore search engines will not show your website in those browsers. Its a good idea to depend on HTML5 for playing audio and video.

Social Sharing

Implement social sharing buttons in you website. Till will increase your websites social activity. Search engines does consider social activity while calculating authority. You can use popular services like AddThis to implement social buttons on your website.

Spelling and Grammar

Make sure that you don't have spelling or grammar in your webpage. Search engines don't like these errors. So we can say spelling and grammar errors make a affect on page authority.

Guest Posting

Many people do guest posting to increase number of backlinks. Search engines are smart enough to recognise these links and they don't increase page authority anymore.

Use of themes

There is absolutely no negative impact of using themes to build your website. Many websites can have the same design and look.

Domain age

Domain age has no impact in search ranking. Therefore don't worry about domain age. Try to put quality content in your website.

Paid Backlinks

Search engines don't like paid backlinks. If they find out about this then they will consider your website to be spam.

14

SEO Tools

In this chapter I will introduce some handy SEO tools which will help to maintain your website SEO and also provide SEO guidance.

Open Site Explorer

Its a online tool which will help you to find the back links of your competitor websites. Therefore you can use their strategy to survice and complete with them.

This tool also calculates page authority and provides all other kinds information about inbound links.

You can find open site explorer at http://www.opensiteexplorer.org/.

Google Webmaster Tools

Google webmaster tools are a set of tools provided by google to help website owners to optimise and track their website's SEO progress. It would take a whole book to discuss about all the webmaster tools. You can visit webmaster tools at https://www.google.com/webmasters/tools/ and explore everything.

Google Data Highlighter

Google data highlighter is one of the Google webmaster tools. Using Google data highlighter you can explicitly tell Google about the content in your website.

Visit Google data highlighter site at https://www.google.com/webmasters/tools/data-highlighter.

SEO SiteCheckup

SEO SiteCheckup is a free online tool using which you can check your website's SEO problems. It reports problems related to basic SEO, compressions, server side, mobile ready and social sharing.

SEO sitecheckup tool is available at skillfeed.com.

robots.txt generator

robots.txt is a online tool using which you can generate a robots.txt file.

You can find this tool at http://www.yellowpipe.com/yis/tools/robots.txt/.

Google Analytics

Google Analytics is a service offered by Google that generates detailed statistics about a website's traffic and traffic sources and measures conversions and sales.

Using this tool you can track how users are navigating through your website therefore you can make improvements accordingly.

Check this tool at http://www.google.com/analytics/.

Copyscape

Copyscape serves both as a plagiarism checker and a duplicate-content checker. Great to use if your content has been distributed across the web.

Check this tool at http://www.copyscape.com/

Siteliner

Using siteliner you can find duplicate content in your website and therefore make using of canonical link element. Its a very useful tool.

Check this tool at http://www.siteliner.com/

GetListed

This awesome local SEO tool scores your local SEO visibility and gives you actionable next steps to raise your score.

Check this tool at https://getlisted.org/.

Google PageSpeed Insights

Tools, data, and insights to improve your page speed. Page speed is correlated with better rankings and user engagement, so this matters.

Check this tool at https://developers.google.com/speed/pagespeed/insights.

Pingdom

Pingdom offers an entire suite of speed tools to help analyze page load, DNS issues, and connectivity.

Check this tool at http://tools.pingdom.com/fpt/.

URI Valet

A great tool for digging into server headers, canonical information, analyzing redirect problems and more.

Check this tool at http://urivalet.com/.

About The Author

Since 2012, Narayan Prusty has been a SEO specialist and a web developer. He is gained experience while working with large number of clients and companies. He spends most of the time doing research on Internet marketing. He loves blogging, you can subscribe to his blog at qnimate.com.

He also spends his time doing research on Big data and CMS. He loves the way web works and therefore we wants to make other to love the web.

You can follow him on Twitter: @narayanprusty

www.ingramcontent.com/pod-product-compliance
Lightning Source LLC
Chambersburg PA
CBHW041101180526
45172CB00001B/51